How the Dog Helps

poems by

Revey Hertzler

Finishing Line Press
Georgetown, Kentucky

How the Dog Helps

Copyright © 2020 by Revey Hertzler
ISBN 978-1-64662-147-7 First Edition
All rights reserved under International and Pan-American Copyright Conventions. No part of this book may be reproduced in any manner whatsoever without written permission from the publisher, except in the case of brief quotations embodied in critical articles and reviews.

ACKNOWLEDGMENTS

Special thanks to Kenny, for convincing me I needed a dog in my life, and to my publisher, for believing my dog is worth reading about.

Publisher: Leah Maines

Editor: Christen Kincaid

Cover Art: Revey Hertzler

Author Photo: Revey Hertzler

Cover Design: Elizabeth Maines McCleavy

Printed in the USA on acid-free paper.
Order online: www.finishinglinepress.com
　　　　　also available on amazon.com

　　　　　　　　Author inquiries and mail orders:
　　　　　　　　　　Finishing Line Press
　　　　　　　　　　　P. O. Box 1626
　　　　　　　　　Georgetown, Kentucky 40324
　　　　　　　　　　　　U. S. A.

Table of Contents

The Dog Watches 1

Trust 2

Half Lie 3

Anxiety 4

Verbal Abuse 5

Empathy 6

Separation Issues 7

Riot 8

Winter People 9

Connection 10

I Prefer Cats 11

Selfish Bastard 12

Repetition 13

Lost in Translation 14

Therapy, I 15

Nightmares 16

The Concept of Mourning 17

Therapy, II 18

Survival 19

Into the Woods 20

It's a Miracle 21

Therapy, III 22

Pivot 23

Indigo 24

How the Dog Helps 25

For the dog

The dog watches.
    Les montres de chien.

We stood loosely and without definition
on the sun-bleached boards of our roof
and despite the big white orb she stared straight up,
tracking across the February expanse
a heart-shaped balloon as it drifted off
someplace to curl into itself and die.

Today I ran through an intersection while the walk sign was on.
I drank coffee fast, swallowed it down with French grammar
and stared for a very long time at a black cursor.
I saw nothing but a daily habit.

She saw the dust motes and the moths,
the finches on the stoop of the library,
the life that persisted around us and I think
the fresh scar in my soul.

It was a helicopter tonight.
The wind cut through my sleeves and
I kept calling out to her, a shadow in the distance:
Hurry, Dog.
Instead she stopped for ten seconds and
watched the helicopter with soft eyes,
the red and green and sputtering circle of the blades.

Trust

When she was a puppy I gave her a lemon wedge.
She might have been a bear cub,
rounded and black, teeth sharp as needles.
That day she'd punctured a hole in my water bottle,
pulled fur from the cat,
frayed a shoelace,
clawed an ankle.

I gave her a lemon wedge out of spite.
She took it, grateful, into the kitchen,
where she dropped it and shook her head.
Then she pinched it between her teeth and
took it to the dining room:
Dropped it, shook her head.
Tried again but went only a step:
Dropped it, frowned as if outside my guilt
she were capable of frowning.
Finally she bowed low and
danced circles around it until
she grew tired and curled up at my feet,
as if she'd decided what I'd given her
wasn't a treat, but a toy.
As if I couldn't possibly have given it to her
out of anything but love.

Half Lie

The breeder lied, you know.
It was eight hours from home to her place so we
both drove four and met in the middle of nowhere.
How'd she do on the drive? I'd asked.
Fine, said the breeder.
She didn't think I'd have any problems.

It was a half lie.
The dog slept soundly the last four
but cried in my bedroom until sunrise.

Anxiety

Dog's got anxiety, needs medication.
She's excitable, intractable,
sits unsettled beside the world.

I'm afraid she thinks this place
will devour her if she doesn't
give it her heart and all her sanity,
that if she stills for even a second
she'll fly off its face as it turns.

Last night the alley below my window was loud.
It was two a.m., crushing dark, and the Hostile Human was back.
I don't mind calling her that because

she harasses residents and
screams bloody murder and
she's been dragged away by the cops
more times than I have fingers
but this is the spot she likes and
it's the one she finds her way back to.

(Someone put a couch out there for her,
chocolate leather with visible abrasions,
the whole thing yellow inside like cake.)

She returned at two a.m. and I was already high strung,
curled up on my futon like a macaroni noodle.
I think I'm anxious, too.

Verbal Abuse

Joy, HH is back again.
The dog is on the floor at my feet and
every so often she lifts her chin to
gnaw on my lamp cord,
probably to drown out the screams.

I use my toes to push her chin back down
and then distract her with a neck massage.
She loves those, they calm her.
Am I encouraging bad behavior?
Am I the couch in the alley?

I can't bear to move her, the dog.
She's warm, it calms me.
I wonder if verbal abuse
calms the couch lender,
if to them it feels like home.

Empathy

I do a lot in the bath.
Sometimes I plan the day, sometimes I pull my knees to my chest and
press my head against the running faucet. There are times
I blow out a breath and sink, and other times
I watch starving polar bears or the journey of an almond.
Sometimes I count bubbles but often I just panic.

I take a lot of baths, and I've recently started trusting the dog
enough to stay in the room with me.
She's got to be watched, you see,
or else she has to go to her crate.
If she's not in her crate she eats my retainers.

She still bothers me here.
(I do a lot in the bathtub, sometimes I write.)
At first she was afraid the bath was for her.
It took a few days for that fear to pass.

She then tried to drink the hot water.
Later she tore a thread from my bath rug,
a stick from the wicker basket.
If the toilet isn't shut her head disappears.
If my underwear isn't in the hamper she'll eat it.

Now that we've had a few weeks of practice she mostly stares at me
for long periods of time or tries to lick the shampoo bottles.
The other day, when my thoughts had a grip on my sanity,

she stretched out her neck to rest her head on my chest.
I rubbed her ear and we both stared forlornly at the wall.

Separation Issues

Tonight I wanted to put on vinyl
to have some noise other than the keyboard
and the awful *whip-whipping* of the dryer, but the record didn't spin.

The other day I'd tested the dog's ability to be left alone by
keeping the bathroom door open while I bathed.

I thought she was ready.
I thought she'd done fine,

but it appears her anxiety chewed right through my favorite album.

Riot

The dog isn't the only one in this place who hates to be left alone.
I haven't been alone since I was twelve.
She hasn't been alone since she was born.
I had my lovers and she had her tattered fleece blankets.
Neither were all that different.
I got married and she got a brand-new blanket,
but we both still riot unattended.

Winter People

We no longer live in the place she was raised.
She grew up on the prairie, east of the badlands and north of Fargo.
She was born in winter, like me, and I think we both were made for it.

We're in a studio flat in the hot city now. I'm chasing a paycheck and
she's chasing cats and motorcycles, delivery boys and shadows.
If she had a tail she'd chase that, too.

Not much has changed and still everything has.
We're the same but our winter is gone.

Connection

The dog has to be touched constantly:
the ear, the nose, the shoulder blade, the toenail.

I'm less demanding but just as desperate:
the scalp, the knee, the forearm, the brain.

I Prefer Cats

I've never been much of a dog person,
always liked cats better.

Cats get it:
Give me space, groom yourself, be reasonable about loving me.

Something about dogs always rubbed me wrong:
the voice, the blind faith, the incessant need for companionship.

Everything I hate about dogs I hate about myself.
I'm not much of a dog person but I'm not too fond of me, either.

Selfish Bastard

The dog loves children.
Maybe it's because
they're harmless
but probably not.
She's excitable and children
are capsules of excitement.
They love the world like she does:
stupidly, uninformed.
She feeds off smiles, eye contact,
hands out, palms up.
These are invitations to love
endlessly and she has no clue how to not.
The dog loves children without knowing what they are, or…
Or maybe she knows exactly and I've got it upside down.

I don't want kids.
I've been on the fence
since I saw one die
but it's mostly my
ego that decided.
I just don't want them.
I want to get baked and watch The Matrix,
sleep in late and have sex on a balcony in Cannes
and then miss my flight home on purpose.
I want to move through life taking my time and
I want to feed it into slots that better serve me.
I'm a selfish bastard and the dog wants to love all the children.

Repetition

Part of the annoyance is that I have to repeat things constantly.
I know experts say not to do that, but I can't help myself.
Do not eat that. Leave it.
Leave it. Do not eat that.
Part of the relief is that she obviously hears me.
Not yet, smells good, glad you're here though.
I grew up repeating myself when no one was listening.
This must be some kind of progress.

Lost in Translation

The dog sneezed and I blessed her.
I sneezed and the dog tackled me for fear I was dying.

Therapy, I

Neither of us likes loud noises.
For me it's the mufflers,
the car alarms they trigger
that trigger my unease.
She picked up on this and
took to leaning against
my thigh as I bear it.
She doesn't much like
big diesel engines,
buckles at the roar, so I learned to
hold a treat to her nose 'til they pass,
to forcibly remind her of
how good the world can taste.

Nightmares

The dog was having a nightmare.
She was halfway under the futon and twitching,

I was halfway atop it, jamming my fingers to make sense of thought.
I rubbed her with the heel of my foot and she woke,

charged and oblivious to her recent suffering.
She crawled up next to me and sighed over my keyboard
the same time I did.

No more nightmares, I told us.

The Concept of Mourning

The couch in the alley is gone,
someone ate the cake.
HH is gone too, but she'll be back.

I feel bad for the dog at the thought of HH's return—
her bed is in the corner closest to the howls.

The first time the dog heard grief was during a movie.
Lolita was devastated and she crawled into bed with
Humbert Humbert for false security.

I didn't like the sound because I was all too familiar with it.
The dog didn't like it because she wasn't,

she cried along with her.
Weird, the Hostile Human becoming a regular part of her life

when Humbert Humbert was the one to introduce her to
the concept of mourning.

HH & HH. Lenders and givers and dealers of heartbreak.

Therapy, II

It isn't easy to cry with this dog,
this battery, this generator of unyielding love.
The other night I found myself folded in half
on the living room floor and
before my grief announced itself
she threw her entire body on top of mine and had
an unbelievable episode of desperate revival.
She might have thought she could beg the sorrow away.
For all the distraction it might have worked.

I was down for six days,
sick the first half and depressed the second.
I survived off butter and when I finally
mustered the strength to walk the dog (poor dog),
she licked my hand the whole way.
She nudged it at stoplights and even past buses,
well beyond her distractible phobia of them.

I think the dog knows feelings.
She's looked at me so often lately with
eyes that might as well say *poor human*.

One doesn't eat well when depressed,
but I've been coming up out of its lethargy.
This afternoon I sat scrolling through
hashtag-dogs-of-Instagram and there was
a video of two Aussies eating carrots.

Alexa: Can dogs eat carrots?
There was a week-old bag in the fridge,
organic, untouched
(one doesn't eat well when depressed).
I was curious if she'd like it.
I was hopeful she'd be happy.
Last minute I rinsed off two,
figuring she might trust it more
if I ate one with her.

Survival

The days
have been hard,
too hard,
that liquor or
gravestone
kind of hard.

Is that the cost of living?
You pay it or it eats you.
It eats you 'til you pay it.

The dog and I were in bed,
she at my feet and I
in the wrinkles of my brain.
It was the throb of her heartbeat
against the sole of my foot.
That's all it took to pull me
from those cracks and deposit me
back onto the path of remembrance,
the path of things worth survival.

Into the Woods

The city was hard on us both,
        but now we've come to the woods.

We've come to the woods and unloaded
        our discontented minds onto the frozen lakes,

the slick mudbanks where necks of Canadian geese
        disappear between their shoulder blades.

We've come after packing, discarding,
        then waving goodbye to the browbeaten

sample of humanity that's lived
        too long amongst too few trees,

those pale drunk faces that waved back
        from their barstools on Main Street.

It's a Miracle

I'm out of the smog and
less of a studio-depressive.

The dog, too.

There should be studies about this.
There should be swells of our population

gone back to the forest.

Therapy, III

She went wild.
We've favorited late summer,
when the fields are still soft and the days long.

I had set her free
on the trail behind our house
and she bounced like rubber through the cattails,

chased a deer,
delivered the long stump
of a fallen pine as if I could throw it,

as if she recalled
the lemon and gave pranking a whirl.
Her ambition returned as if it were never gone,

her anxiety melted
as if it were the remnants of a dream.

Pivot

There are pivotal moments in life.
As I sit here in the grass

throwing a ball for a dog who knows it's spring,
watching the blackbirds dance aggressively in the sky

as if their life depends on ritual,
and as I think about the time I almost died,

it dawns on me that it's possible
to have pivoted and to have missed it.

Suddenly I feel,
as the trees creak like floorboards in the wind

just as they did this time last year,
and as the dog's boredom manifests itself as vomited grass

as it does after every thaw,
that I'm now faced in a blinding new direction.

Indigo

We walk.
We walk mounds risen in the bluegrass,
trip holes dug deep by flickertails.

We walk borders,
count fence posts,
grind pavement with the soles of our weary feet.

We walk miles away from sunrise,
straight into dusk, cloak ourselves in indigo and wonder
about shadows, the undefined edges of returning darkness.

We walk distances back to our fret,
bodies earth-trodden and dark with soil,
hairs branching out like the naked limbs of our favorite maple tree.

How the Dog Helps

The dog, she can't help it,
she pursues: mail men, laser dots, love.

Today it was a snow hare, large and wispy, the color of dead-fire smoke.
She chased it 'til the leash went from my hand,
chased it across the field and over the hill.

When I came down I saw her, poised,
eyes trained on a couple walking past.

Her gaze met mine, overeager, as if to welcome my presence,
as if to tell me all about the great swell that had hit her heart.

I saw the shift in the white of her eyes,
the indication that her course had changed.

Before I could warn her, before I could warn them,
to disarm them of their panic

at the sight of a black form hurling their direction, she abandoned the
hare and sprinted with all her might in pursuit of new friendship.

The man stiffened, the woman hunched,
then the man, the man braced.

I shouted something like *Service dog!*
but my words fell dead in the space between us.

I watched her as she reached them, ears back, eyes wide,
about to crouch to the ground,

about to greet, to invite, to submit,
but with no tail to show for it.

They didn't see what I saw.
They just saw black in motion.

The man, he lifted his foot and swung to kick her,
kicked her hard, straight in the head,

and then he locked his arms around her body
to contain a threat that was never really there.

She was scared, and why not?
They were scared first, and that's all it takes.

This is what we'd run from,
this brutality of life,
of human interaction,
a darkness we'd hoped to escape,

and now I was running towards it, running fast, running breathless.
She yelped, spun her head to bite at the restraint across her rib cage.

Don't, I thought, only that,
and then he raised an arm, ready to strike,

ready to oppress her, to pound from her
the spirit she'd somehow maintained
through all the grime of the world,
the fundamental trust she always dispensed

back into it, the love that had saved me,
and saved me,
and saved me…

So I hit him first,
hit him hard,

straight in the gut to shock him into release.
Then I tried harder, all that I owed to her concentrated in my hands

bound for a man who now represented
everything wrong with the world,
the Man Afraid, the fear-driven, the judgmental,
and all the nuanced mistakes

and injustices suspended like specks of glass in the web of our society,
hamstringing what dreams and compassion should try to pass.

So I hit him, and hit him, angry, angrier still,
wrath coming, hate coming, down and down

upon the big wrong world the dog had forgiven,
and forgiven,
and forgiven.

Revey Hertzler is a writer and environmentalist from Pensacola, Florida. While working towards a degree in English and Creative Writing she completed her first screenplay, which went on to earn her a year-long fellowship with an entertainment company in New York. She began *How the Dog Helps* in Los Angeles while working in the film industry and completed it in North Dakota. She currently works in the nonprofit sector and is a grant writer for the Red Cross. You can follow her @realrevey or visit www.realrevey.com.

www.ingramcontent.com/pod-product-compliance
Lightning Source LLC
LaVergne TN
LVHW041512070426
835507LV00012B/1507